WORK AND BUSINESS

[
Career and Work
Starting a Business
]

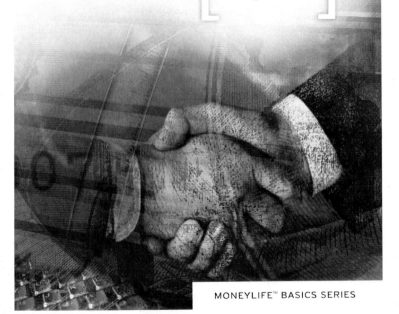

MONEYLIFE™ BASICS SERIES

ISBN 978-1-56427-254-6

Verses identified as (NIV) are taken from the *Holy Bible: New International Version*, ©1973, 1978, 1984 by the International Bible Society. Used by permission of Zondervan Bible Publishers.

Verses identified as (TLB) are taken from *The Living Bible*, ©1971 by Tyndale House Publishers, Wheaton, Illinois. Used by permission.

All other Scripture quotations are taken from the *New American Standard Bible®* (Updated Edition) (NASB), ©1960, 1962, 1963, 1968, 1971, 1972, 1973, 1975, 1977, 1995 by The Lockman Foundation. Used by permission.

MoneyLife™ is a trademark of Crown Financial Ministries.

For inquiries in Canada, please contact CrownCanada.ca or call 1-866-401-0626.

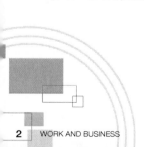

July 2008 Edition

CONTENTS

INTRODUCTION

If you work—or expect to in the future—this book offers help, hope and insight regarding one of the greatest investments of your life. Since you will spend roughly half of your waking hours in some kind of work, it is vitally important to make informed, thoughtful decisions that will affect your effectiveness as well as your financial and emotional rewards.

Are you content to spend thousands of hours in an unfulfilling routine that trades drudgery for the dollars you need to survive? Or would you rather engage in work that is meaningful to you and provides a sense of accomplishment? The same job can fit either description; it all depends on how it fits you.

This book will help you if you are:

- considering a career change,

- a student preparing for a first career,

- thinking about starting your own business,

- unfulfilled at work and wondering about other options you would enjoy more, or

- wanting to be more productive in your current work environment.

Investing a few hours in this book and its associated resources could change your career path and your life. Modern technology is often about speed, tempting us to think we should be able to do everything quickly. Life's most important issues, however, are seldom single events; they are processes that take time, effort and commitment.

Choosing and building a career is one of these.

Counselors are taught not to make decisions for clients, even though clients may want them to. People implement decisions far better when they process good counsel and draw their own conclusions. We want to help you do that as you move through the various stages of your career—whether as an employee or entrepreneur.

If you have not yet completed our *Career Direct® Complete Guidance System* assessment, we encourage you to complete it online at CareerDirectOnline.org. It reveals your God-given pattern for work and a good description of the type of work for which you are best suited, without attempting to tell you exactly what to do. You'll also find a free *Personality ID®* profile that gives you a small glimpse of the power of finding more than a career but a true calling for your life.

As you work toward choosing and building a career, we urge you to follow an effective formula: Pray for guidance, work the process, and trust God for the results. These three steps help you to acknowledge God's role and find peace as you faithfully do your part. We are confident of God's confirmation on a career pathway that honors Him. *"I am the light of the world; he who follows me will not walk in the darkness, but will have the Light of life"* (John 8:12).

Help and Hope Are Here.

Crown exists to provide help, hope, and insight. These Help and Hope buttons appear whenever special information is available to assist and encourage you.

Please notice a few helpful features we include in every *MoneyLife™ Basics Series* book.

1. Appendix 1 is an introduction to Christ. If you (or someone you know) are uncertain about where you stand with God, this short introduction will guide you into an intimate relationship with Him.

2. Appendix 2, "God's Ownership & Financial Faithfulness," briefly explores a fundamental concept—one that frames the correct perspective on every financial principle in Scripture. If you don't understand this, you are likely to manage your resources with worldly wisdom. The world's approach to money management isn't always evil, but it is short-sighted (ignoring eternity), incomplete (ignoring the Creator/Controller/Provider), and usually in pursuit of the wrong goals.

3. Because we are committed to transformation rather than mere information, each chapter ends with a two-part exercise:

   • An Action Step you create based on your response to the chapter

   • A Celebration Plan for every Action Step completed

Please take advantage of these to maximize your experience in this small book. James 1:22 sums it up when it says, *"Do not merely listen to the word, and so deceive yourselves. Do what it says"* (NIV).

CHAPTER 1

CAREER AND WORK

Work will occupy a significant part of your life, and it will affect every other part of your life. Your choice of career and the effort you put into preparing for it can position you to experience great enjoyment in your work even when it is difficult. Many people, however, are unfulfilled in their job while others, doing the same job, find it rewarding. Why?

One obvious reason is that some people choose—or accept—jobs for which they are not well matched. But there is often another factor involved: a basic discontentment that grows out of not having a biblical perspective on work. Our culture has drifted toward a secular view of work—a view that allows us to think we can separate our work from our spiritual life.

This flaw in logic has led to much of the misery we see now in the workplace. As in other areas of life, when we operate with unsound concepts, we suffer the consequences.

In our early days as a nation, even those who were not devout Christians had a concept of a divine calling in their work. In general, work was seen in a more honorable light—as a way to fulfill our purpose in life.

Chuck Colson, founder of Prison Fellowship, wrote, "God created human beings in His own image and part of being 'in His image' means that we are workers—like God Himself. That's where that innate, inner drive for work comes from. Work is part of God's nature."

Although at one time work may have been considered a calling, it now seems to be merely a means to an end. Today's workers believe their labor allows them to purchase pleasure, to fulfill materialistic needs, and to build their egos by gaining power and position. The view was very different in early America, when William Perkins preached that "a person's vocation is a certain kind of life ordained by God and imposed on man for the common good."

Looking at Work from a Biblical Perspective

"For what is a man profited if he gains the whole world, and loses or forfeits himself?" (Luke 9:25).

So, it would be good to begin the career-decision process by taking a look at the errors and the truths that relate to work. If operating under false beliefs is causing so much stress and heartache, then the truth should set us free to find the joy in work that our Creator intended. Let's look first at some of the errors and the problems they cause.

Materialism (Greed)

Probably the biggest deception regarding work in our society today is the belief that a higher income (more money) can bring happiness. Many adults have jobs and are making adequate money, yet they are not fulfilled. Many say without hesitation that they pursued their present careers because those careers offered prestige and high incomes. Now they see the mistake in making decisions based primarily on income. Money does not provide satisfaction.

We hear movie stars, athletes, and other high income celebrities say the same thing. In an interview with *World Wide Challenge* (Campus Crusade for Christ) magazine, Christopher Parkening, one of the preeminent virtuosos of the classical guitar, said it well:

"The world tells you that success is having a lot of money, being famous and being independent—doing what you want to do, when you want to do it.

"For years I pursued success in the music field to the point that I was able to retire to a Montana ranch at age 30. My wife and I were living what most would consider the ideal life. But a year after I got everything I wanted, it meant absolutely nothing. I was empty inside.

"During that period of time I became a Christian, and my priorities changed. When I came across the passage in 1 Corinthians that says, 'Whatever you do, do all for the glory of God,' I realized there were only two things I knew how to do. One was fly fish and the other was play the guitar.

"I went back to playing the guitar, but this time with a different purpose. As Bach once said, 'The aim and final reason of all music is none else but the glory of God.'"

Pride

A second problem is pride. Too much concern with what others think is a "successful" job or a "good position," can lead people to feel ashamed to do what God has gifted them for. Sometimes they burn themselves out trying to do jobs they were not naturally designed to do. You can call it going against the grain, not following your bent, or swimming upstream, but the bottom line is that it's impossible to be excellent for very long when you're not using the talents and strengths God has given you. *"For You formed my inward parts; You wove me in my mother's womb. . . . I am fearfully and wonderfully made"* (Psalm 139:13-14).

Many people are in the wrong jobs because of their parents' pride. As young people, they were pushed into career fields so they could "be somebody" or "amount to something." It's unfortunate when parents want to fulfill their own worldly dreams and boost their egos through their children.

Jesus reprimanded the Pharisees for their preoccupation with impressing men with their outward appearances (reputations). God is concerned with what is inside—the motivation of the heart (character).

Jesus called the Pharisees "hypocrites" because they cleaned the outside of the cup and dish but inside they were full of greed and self-indulgence. He wanted them to clean the inside of the cup and dish (motivation to serve others), and then the outside also would be clean (see Matthew 23:25-26).

Hebrews 13:5 takes it a step further, cautioning against improper financial motivation: *"Make sure that your character is free from the love of money, being content with what you have."*

Even in the Old Testament God made it clear that His evaluation frequently differs from ours. When He chose to anoint David rather than one of his older, taller, more handsome brothers, He reminded Samuel that *"...God sees not as man sees, for man looks at the outward appearance, but the LORD looks at the heart"* (1 Samuel 16:7).

Our pride, often wrapped up in appearances, can be dangerous. *"Pride goes before destruction, and a haughty spirit before stumbling. It is better to be humble in spirit with the lowly than to divide the spoil with the proud"* (Proverbs 16:18-19).

Lack of Trust (Faith)

A third problem in our pursuit of a rewarding career pathway is a lack of trust that God is sufficient for all our needs. We are driven to achieve success so we can eventually gain control of our circumstances and be independent (protected) from the problems of life. This reflects a fundamental error in our thinking, because there is no security in this world. Achievement, more independence, more money, more power—these will never insulate us from life's losses, and there is never enough.

Our only guarantees are God's promises and the assurance of His presence with us in any circumstance He allows in our life: *"...He Himself has said, 'I will never desert you, nor will I ever forsake you'"* (Hebrews 13:5). We must walk each day in faith, depending on Him for every breath.

To make sure we understand how important our faith is to God, Hebrews 11:6 makes this bold statement: *"Without faith it is impossible to please Him, for he who comes to God must believe that He is and that He is a rewarder of those who seek Him."*

The problem is that most of us don't really trust God to be involved personally in our lives, and we miss out on His perfect plan. This is remedied as we grow in our knowledge of God, trading our limited perspective for one that is closer to reality. We recognize that His unlimited power and unconditional love do not always give us what we want; what we want is often deficient. Instead, He gives us what we need and works all things together for good, enabling us to confidently yield and experience His peace.

Jesus described this perfectly in His analogy of the vine and branches: *"I am the vine, you are the branches; he who abides in Me and I in him, he bears much fruit, for **apart from Me you can do nothing**"* (John 15:5, emphasis added).

Ignorance

A final reason for poor career decisions is ignorance. Many people take available jobs just because they have never been taught how to make career decisions. Our culture—particularly churches, schools, and government—offers very little guidance for making career choices.

This book, along with the resources it mentions, will help you leapfrog from ignorance to knowledge that can pay off for the rest of your life.

What Are Some Truths About Work?

God Works

Chapter one of Genesis documents God's work in creating the universe. Furthermore, the entire Bible documents God's work as Lord and Ruler of the universe. We see His work as He protected His people from the Pharaoh on their journey out of Egypt. We see His work as He looked after individuals like David and Daniel. He continues to work in a personal way, assuring us that He cares enough even to number the hairs on our heads. God is obviously not neglecting His work of being God.

Christ was directly involved in the creation and, though fully God, He became fully man and worked on this earth. Apparently Jesus was involved in common labor and, even in the height of His ministry was never employed by the temple. Finally, Jesus carried out His most significant work as a suffering servant—at the cross, obeying the will of the Father.

God Commissioned Work

If we are created in God's image, then we also are divinely ordained for work. Genesis 1:26-30 details our role in work: We rule over the lower creation.

God commissioned Adam to work in the sinless perfection of Eden. *"Then the Lord God took the man and put him into the garden of Eden to cultivate it and keep it"* (Genesis 2:15). Work is not a punishment for sin; it was—and remains to this day—a divine gift with a potential for self-expression that is unique to humankind. The entrance of sin in the world merely complicated work and made it more difficult.

Because God created us as moral beings, our work and its products can be used for good or evil. Yet the clear implication throughout the Bible is that work is part of the divine nature and, therefore, should bring glory to our Creator.

Our Talents Glorify God

It honors the Father when we are true to our creation. Ralph Mattson and Arthur Miller make this point quite well in their book, *Finding a Job You Can Love* (Thomas Nelson Publishers). "We please God when we act the way we are designed to act, when we are who God designed us to be. When such actions are carried out with the intention of being expressions of love to Him, they do in fact become expressions of love to Him."

Consider this example of being faithful to God's design. Jeremy Burton wanted to be a youth leader and work in the area of recreation or at the YMCA. Instead, he became a computer programmer because his parents told him he needed to make more money and be more successful.

By his late 20s he had burned out on his successful job. His career assessment clearly revealed how God had equipped him to be an encourager and leader of youth. He made a career change, and his life has taken on new meaning as a YMCA leader. He is excited because he is getting to do what he was designed to do.

Can you imagine a bluebird trying to be a woodpecker just so it can attract more attention? His bill is not equipped for drilling holes. A bluebird honors its

Creator by being a very beautiful blue-bird. Likewise, those who recognize their talents and use them for the glory of God become a magnificent testimony to the work of the Creator. *"Whether then, you eat or drink or whatever you do, do it all to the glory of God"* (1 Corinthians 10:31).

In their book, *Your Work Matters to God* (Navpress), Doug Sherman and Bill Hendricks provide an in-depth look at the biblical view of work. They point out that the workplace provides more than mere income for our provision and tithe; it is also a primary place for our witness. Ministry is not the work of full-time professionals; it is the work of full-time followers of Christ—all of us. *"There are varieties of ministries, and the same Lord"* (1 Corinthians 12:5).

Parents Are Called to Nurture

Not everyone has to earn a paycheck to fulfill their calling. For example, a mother's call to bear and nurture children takes priority over other career considerations. In a culture where career choice is driven by materialism, many mothers believe they must have a career in order to be fulfilled. But fulfillment comes from knowing we are in God's will by carrying out His purpose for our lives.

Scripture does not preclude mothers from being employed outside the home, but the high value it places on parenting and home management may preclude a "normal" career while children are young. God has clearly gifted women as family nurturers, both physically and emotionally.

The need for love and quality instruction for children in the home resides with both parents. A parent's role is the most important one in our society. If parents fails, society fails. Both a mother and father provide essential elements of sacrificial love and support. Many of society's most vexing problems are a direct result of parents becoming overly committed to work and leisure, at the expense of nurturing their children.

We recommend the *Career Direct® Complete Guidance System* for all parents and especially for spouses who are full-time homemakers. Stay-at-home parents will be able to do their jobs better at home if they know their pattern of strengths and struggles. Then, if homemakers later decide to pursue outside careers, the assessment will help them choose vocations—and associated educational and training tracks—which highlight their strengths.

Our Work Can Advance the Great Commission

We are to be blessings to others. We can trace this commission to the Old Testament and God's covenant with Abram in Genesis 12:2-3 where He says, *"I will bless you . . . and in you all the families of the earth will be blessed."* We are descendants of Abram, branches through which God's blessings flow.

We are to be lights to the world. *"In Him was life, and the life was the Light of men"* (John 1:4). He told us, *"You are the light of the world. A city set on a hill cannot be hidden; nor does anyone light a lamp and put it under a bushel, but on the lampstand, and it gives light to all who are in the house"* (Matthew 5:14-15).

As followers of Jesus Christ, we are to be different. His Spirit is in us, producing the light that attracts others to Him.

"Let your light shine before men in such a way that they may see your good works, and glorify your Father who is in heaven" (Matthew 5:16).

If our work is meant to reflect God's light, we need a better motivation than greed or human pride, which reflect nothing more than the desires of fallen humankind. Our work is sacred and must be done to honor and glorify God. Ultimately, our attitudes and performance at work will either honor Him or detract from Him.

We are to live by truth. We pray that as you go through this book, you will come face to face with your Creator and gain a new perspective on His truths regarding work. If you are like most of us, this will be a painful, yet liberating, experience. The pain comes from confronting our past sinful motivations, but we can take joy in knowing He forgives and does not remember our selfish past.

Perhaps you have made some career mistakes due to errors in thinking. If so, you can be like the apostle Paul, who personified this attitude: *"...One thing I do: forgetting what lies behind and reaching forward to what lies ahead, I press on toward the goal for the prize of the upward call of God in Christ Jesus"* (Philippians 3:13-14).

The foundation for all career planning is the biblical principle that everything we do is ultimately for God and His purposes. As we are able to trust God in this important area of our lives, He increases our faith and reveals or confirms career pathways that will bring Him glory, honor, and praise; and that's the best of all possible outcomes of our work.

"He who practices the truth comes to the Light, so that his deeds may be manifested as having been wrought in God" (John 3:21).

Biblical Principles of the Career Planning Process

1. **We are unique creations of God.** *"You formed my inward parts; You wove me in my mother's womb. I will give thanks to You, for I am fearfully and wonderfully made; wonderful are Your works, and my soul knows it very well"* (Psalm 139:13-14).

2. **God blesses us individually with spiritual gifts that are also work-related talents.** *"Since we have gifts that differ according to the grace given us, each of us is to exercise them accordingly: if prophecy, according to the proportion of his faith; if service, in his serving; or he who teaches, in his teaching; or he who exhorts, in his exhortation; he who gives, with liberality; he who leads, with diligence; he who shows mercy, with cheerfulness"* (Romans 12:6-8).

3. **Excellence in our work broadens our platform for influence.** *"Do you see a man skilled in his work? He will stand before kings; he will not stand before obscure men"* (Proverbs 22:29).

4. **Our larger calling, evidenced in the workplace, is to be witnesses and lights to the world.** This is greatly enhanced when we are experiencing the joy of using our talents at work. *"Let*

*your light shine before men in
such a way that they may see your
good works, and glorify your Father
who is in heaven"* (Matthew 5:16).

 ## *Making Career Decisions*

Richard Bolles, author of *What Color is Your Parachute?*,
discusses the need to unlearn the errors we have learned and
then learn the truths. That is the purpose of this section. First
we will look at what we need to unlearn about choosing a
career; then we will outline some steps that have proven to be
successful.

How to Make Bad Career Decisions

1. **Choose the first/easiest job you can get.** This is
   an easy approach, but it certainly is not being a good
   steward of your talents. Although there may be times
   when you will need to take an interim job just to put
   food on the table, your goal should always be to move
   into positions where you will exercise your strongest
   talents. *"The soul of the sluggard craves and gets
   nothing, but the soul of the diligent is made fat"* (Proverbs 13:4).

2. **Choose a job based on the amount of money it
   pays.** We have already discussed this, but this error is
   so established in our culture that most people will need
   significant faith to choose a job on any other basis.
   Often, it is the attraction of materialism and our pride
   that causes us to want more and more. *"He who loves*

money will not be satisfied with money, nor he who loves abundance with its income. This too is vanity" (Ecclesiastes 5:10).

3. Choose a job because it sounds like a good title. Have you noticed how companies have changed the names of jobs to make them sound more important? One discount store calls its cashiers "terminal operators," and I'm sure you have noticed the emphasis our society places on having a good position. Doing what you're good at and what you enjoy is usually a far better way to choose a career path than just selecting a title and doing the work that accompanies it.

"Better is he who is lightly esteemed and has a servant than he who honors himself and lacks bread" (Proverbs 12:9).

A friend recently said, "I am fortunate because I love my work. I have variety, I am outdoors, I get to help people, and I'm my own boss." Many people would not want his job, however, because he pumps out septic tanks. We can admire this man for what he does and for the way he honors God in his work. Many people have impressive titles but hate their work and would give anything to love it.

4. Take a job just because management offers it. Although doing your work with excellence often leads to promotions, not every promotion makes sense. This is proven constantly in situations where skilled workers are promoted to management level jobs. They may have excelled in their production work, but it takes a completely different set of abilities and skills to solve people problems, train others to do the work, be responsible for the work of others, meet quotas, and report to higher officials. Far too often the promotion only leads to stress and frustration.

Understanding your work-related attributes—here is where an assessment "pattern" really helps—will enable you and your employer to determine the areas that will be the best fit for you. You may be better off seeking to expand your areas of responsibility in your present job than to move away from your skills and area of expertise.

Don't take a job just because upper management offers it. Many managers still don't comprehend the wisdom of matching people to their work. Upper management might simply be trying to fill a management slot—without serious consideration of whether it matches your talents. Carefully evaluate promotions in light of your God-given strengths and your pattern for work. If it's a match, go for it. If it's not a match, why be promoted to a job that is likely to draw on your areas of weakness and lead to frustration?

5. **Choose a job because that's what your parents do.** Bill Jackson's dad was a chemical engineer and his mom was a biologist. He grew up believing that "real jobs" were to be found in the sciences or law. His

parents never told him that outright; he just assumed it. So the young man struggled to prepare for a career in law. He hated the studies, fought constant discouragement, toiled endlessly for average grades, and finally quit law school. *"The naïve believes everything, but the sensible man considers his steps"* (Proverbs 14:15).

In desperation, Bill used the *Career Direct® Complete Guidance System*, which pointed him toward careers in the arts. He recently graduated with a 4.0 grade average in professional and technical writing. A letter from his college professor attests to his superior qualifications; he was one of the top graduates the department had ever had.

Don't choose a career track just because it's what your parents do. You may be 40 years old and just now discovering the shadow of influence your parents have had on your career planning. God has created you to be unique. Discover that uniqueness and develop your career plans around it.

6. **Choose a job to fulfill your parents' unfulfilled dreams.** Parents sometimes steer their children in a career direction the parents would like. If this is not accompanied by a thorough consideration of the children's God-given pattern, the most likely accomplishment is negative stress.

Even though they don't always show it, young people generally want to please their parents. Many college students delay choosing a major and even suffer clinical depression because they are

unable to resolve a conflict between their parents' desires and their natural bent. Parents need to remember they are not owners; rather, they are stewards, rearing a future adult.

7. **Choose a job just because you have the minimum ability to do it.** God created humans as very special and highly developed organisms, so we all have many basic abilities. We can do many jobs, but they are not necessarily God's plan for us. Usually His plan also involves our highest aptitudes, our greatest skills, our personality strengths and, even more important, our motivations. He causes some areas to appeal to us more than others, and these usually are related to the career field in which He will empower us to shine for Him.

How to Make Good Career Decisions

1. **First clarify your purpose in life.** *"We are God's workmanship, created in Christ Jesus for good works, which God prepared beforehand so that we would walk in them"* (Ephesians 2:10). Followers of Christ must settle a few fundamental questions:

   • Do I really trust my life to God's hands?

   • Am I willing to relinquish control to Him?

   Since God wants what is best for us, and He has shown us over and over that He cares, then why not let Him be in command? Why not commit to being a servant in His kingdom for His honor and glory?

Once you've clarified your purpose, outline some goals based on what you stand for and what you want the end results of your work to be.

2. **Learn about your natural "bent."** This includes your abilities, interests, personality strengths, and your priorities and values. Learning about your bent is the primary purpose of the *Career Direct*® *Complete Guidance System*. A written description of your "pattern" will give you a good picture of your God-given strengths. Understanding how God has gifted you can lead you to your vocation and calling.

3. **Investigate/explore several occupations that fit your "pattern."** Using your pattern, you can concentrate your search on the jobs that potentially are a good fit. Read, interview people, and visit work sites in order to identify jobs that best match your pattern. You have nothing to lose and everything to gain through your efforts. Don't miss out on your niche because you didn't take the time to find it.

Of the many resources available to help you in your search for career information, here are two authoritative ones.

The U.S. Bureau of Labor Statistics publishes the *Occupational Outlook Handbook* (OOH) and many other resources. The OOH is available in hardcover, paperback, and CDROM editions, and it can be found in most libraries and career centers. You can also access it online at http://www.bls.gov/oco. From this site, you also can read articles from *Occupa-*

tional Outlook Quarterly magazine online.

The Occupational Information Network is a comprehensive database of worker attributes and job characteristics. As the replacement for the Dictionary of Occupational Titles (DOT), O*NET is the nation's primary source of occupational information through the U.S. Department of Labor. Explore its many resources at http://www.onetcenter.org.

4. **Seek God's confirmation.** Once you have discovered your "pattern" and glanced through the occupational resources listed in #3, some possibilities should begin to jump out at you. Continue to pray specifically for God's direction in your search and His leading in your decision. *"Delight yourself in the Lord; and he will give you the desires of your heart"* (Psalm 37:4).

   Share your information with other Christians who know you well, and seek their counsel. *"Where there is no guidance the people fall, but in abundance of counselors there is victory"* (Proverbs 11:14). Trust that God will help you make your choice. Wait until He gives you peace about your decision.

5. **Choose your direction and initial destination, and develop a plan to get there.** If necessary, prepare yourself through education and training to reach your goal. *"The plans of the diligent lead surely to advantage, but everyone who is hasty comes surely to poverty"* (Proverbs 21:5). When you develop your talents you are like the servants who invested their talents and

doubled them during the master's absence (see Matthew 25:14-30).

6. **Learn to manage your own career.** Have you thought of your career as a stewardship issue, as the above verse suggests? The pace of change these days is so fast that people must be prepared to change occupations—even careers—more often than a decade or two ago. It is better to anticipate change than to be surprised by it; just ask the person at the back of the line!

How do you spot work trends that might influence your career path? The Internet is the place to begin. You can search for jobs, receive advice on careers and résumés, or research a company you are considering. Entering "career information" into the Google search engine just now yielded over 50 million results in .22 seconds!

Among the best of secular sources on the Web, the following sites are recommended often. They are listed in alphabetical order, not according to preference, with a brief description of what you will find there.

- America's Job Bank, at http://www.ajb.dni.us. This is a partnership between the U.S. Department of Labor and the state operated public Employment Service. Almost 1,000,000 jobs were listed the last time we checked this site.

  - Job Web, at http://www.jobweb.com. Sponsored by the National Association of Colleges and Employers, this site

matches students and alumni
with potential employers.

- The Monster Board, at http://www.monster.com offers résumé management, job search agent, careers network, chats and message boards, advice on career management, and more.

- What Color Is Your Parachute, from Dick Bolles, author of the same titled book, at http://www.jobhuntersbible.com. This site offers up-to-date job search information.

7. **Become a lifelong learner, always gathering new ideas about your work and its related fields.** Our society has moved through the agricultural age, the industrial age, and is now in the information age with farmers using computers and advanced technology to compete. Renowned management consultant Peter Drucker said, "Continuous learning will be the most important thing in the 21st century. Reading, taking courses, and further training are a way of life for those who want to excel at work."

8. **Refine your career as you go along.** After you're in a job, you'll see areas in which you can grow and develop. Prepare to move when doors open. Be careful not to move into an area that does not suit your strengths. We often see employees move into management because it looks like a good career move, only to discover the stress of being mismatched to their new responsibilities.

The Role of Prayer in Decision Making

We cannot leave the subject of decision making without emphasizing the importance of prayer. God has ordained prayer as a powerful way for you to operate in the supernatural spiritual realm on this earth. In prayer, God molds your heart to His perfect will, and it is through prayer that He changes the hearts of others and sometimes even your circumstances. Neglecting prayer is disobedience that shortchanges you of God's best for you.

HOW TO PRAY

1. **Create a prayer agenda for each scheduled prayer time.** This can range from a brief list of names and job leads to more extensive journal notes. As you compile this agenda, don't allow your career issues to consume your entire prayer life. Maintain balance in your devotions by concentrating on God's character, and don't forget to include the needs of others. *"Do not merely look out for your own personal interests, but also for the interests of others"* (Philippians 2:4). As difficult as it may sound, life goes on in spite of your career transition, and God desires to touch the lives of others through you.

2. **File your past prayer agendas.** By keeping track of them, you will be able to see answers to your prayers as time passes. This can become a real source of encouragement to you and your spouse.

3. **Ask God for an open heart to His Word.** *"Many plans are in a man's heart, but the counsel of the Lord will stand"* (Proverbs 19:21). According to Psalm 1, the person who delights in the law of the Lord *"is like a tree firmly planted by streams of water, which yields its fruit in its season and its leaf does not wither; and in whatever he does, he prospers"* (Psalm 1:3). Like seeds sown in a garden, the principles from God's Word will sprout, bearing the fruits of righteousness, peace, and purpose in your life.

4. **Praise God for His faithfulness to you and your family.** If you cannot discern His provision for you, ask Him to show you how He's providing. One of His names is *Jehovah-Jireh*, meaning "Jehovah's provision shall be seen."

WE ALL NEED PRAYER PARTNERS

We are to pray alone, but we also need to have prayer partners. We need the support of our spouses, our families, our friends, and we also need a same-gender prayer partner. There is something very special and very encouraging about a prayer partner. If you don't have one, get one, and meet at least once a week to share and pray together.

A Framework for Decision Making

In coaching sessions at Crown Financial Ministries, we've observed over and over a systematic plan for discovering God's will. This method works for career, financial, or any other type of decision-making situation. As you can see, this is rarely an overnight process; rather, it's a walk of faith.

Too often we work things backward. We decide on the results we want and then pray that God will bless us and make them happen. When we do this we deny Him full control, and we deny ourselves His full blessings. Turning the results over to Him is a critical but necessary step for receiving His best.

Trust - Faith

Our Role—Process	God's Role—Results
• Submit and commit to follow God's call	• Open doors
• Pray for His will and wisdom	• Close doors
• Anticipate the likelihood of change	• Confirm His will
• Work the process—Assessment, résumé, investigation, job search, and so on	• Give us peace
• Seek godly counsel	• Produce results
• Exercise patience—wait	• Glorify His name
• Glorify God	

Holy Spirit

Keys to Employment in the 21st Century

Introduction to Change

The saying goes that there are three kinds of people in the world: those who make something happen, those who watch it happen, and those who never knew it happened.

The cutting edge for workers in the 21st century belongs to those who make things happen. Two key characteristics (which may seem like opposites) describe workers who thrive in this rapidly changing world of work: focus and versatility.

One key element for 21st-century workers is the ability to focus on work that emphasizes their natural strengths and talents. This requires a thorough understanding of how God has gifted them. Workers lacking this typically produce mediocre results while those focusing on their strengths remain highly motivated and excel.

Versatility is the second key to competence. It's not enough to simply know how God has created us. In addition, we must be able to discern quickly how to use our God-given talents in new work settings.

In football, this simple strategy is known as "read and react." Every player on defense pays close attention to changes in the offensive alignment. This is his first clue to necessary adjustments in position. Then when the football is snapped to the quarterback, the defensive player must immediately read where the play is headed so he can be in the right place at the right time to complete his assignment.

Ten Major Trends

Armed with a knowledge of our God-given strengths, 21st-century workers must "read and react" to changes in order to compete. This requires taking initiative for personal career development rather than waiting for employers to see and suggest adjustments.

For this reason, we have compiled a number of major trends that are reshaping the work world around us. As you review them, do your best to discover implications for yourself and your career development.

1. BECOMING A GLOBAL VILLAGE

The close of the 20th century brought about rapid changes in worldwide trade policies, with the ratification of major treaties like NAFTA[1] resulting in a complex, interdependent global market. The United States signed on to the NAFTA and GATT[2] treaties.

No longer operating within independent, nationalistic cultures, the work forces of industrialized and Third World nations have begun to collide. The 350 million high-paid workers in industrialized nations are suddenly competing with over a billion workers in Third World nations who are eager to work for far less. The result has been abrupt changes in trade policy.

Workers who are adept at high tech communications will continue to be in demand. Likewise, those who become proficient in a second or third language will hold the edge in the competitive, global workforce. Increasingly, corporations will

need to grow in knowledge and
sensitivity to once-remote cultures.

2. FURTHER CORPORATE DOWN-SIZING

As global networking increases, market
prices must remain steady in order to stay
competitive. Expect mergers, cost-cutting mea-
sures, and layoffs to continue in an effort to maintain
corporate profits. In addition, the growing and efficient
use of technology will permanently replace many workers. Losses in the manufacturing sector, along with
textiles, farming, and middle-management jobs, will be
substantial.

Particularly vulnerable are middle-management men.
Historically, they have been paid more than women in
similar positions. And, although seniority used to be an
asset, it now may very well be a liability. Since workers
who have remained with the same company for many
years are paid more than those hired more recently,
it's no surprise to see this group first on the chopping
block in the quest for corporate savings.

3. MORE WORK FOR FEWER WORKERS

Fewer laid-off workers will be replaced. Instead, remain-
ing staff will be required to take up the slack, resulting
in a heavier work load. So far, the strategy has worked.
The prevailing view is that corporations exist to create immediate profits for current stockholders, not to
create work for employees or long-term growth for the
company. The tendency in many industries is to retain

a minimum of essential employees and work them until they burn out, at which time those employees will move on to other jobs and be replaced by new workers who may have burned out and moved on from their last jobs.

4. TALENT BECOMES FOCUS FOR JOB SECURITY

Job security has become a relic. In the old workplace model, security came with the company. Not any more. Job security in the future belongs to the worker whose "excellent" skills are in high demand. An employee's productivity and quality makes him or her necessary to the economic success of a business or organization. Since each work day has a direct effect on profitability, workers are judged by their daily contributions.

The job market changes rapidly as new technologies create new employment demands. In the future, you may find yourself doing a job that doesn't even exist now. In such rapidly changing work conditions, security rests in the skilled application of your God-given talents in compatible work settings.

Being mismatched in your work lowers productivity, morale, and often, quality of work—not exactly the description for job security.

5. RAPID ADVANCES IN TECHNOLOGY

Few American workers used a computer on their job 20 years ago. Today, more than half of workers use one. We have seen a steep, steady increase in acceptance of new technology in our homes and in our businesses.

The **S Curve** (below) demonstrates how quickly technological advances can be accepted. In history, we have seen this proven with the telephone, television, fax machine, cell phone, computer, and the Internet. As new technologies are introduced, competition will recognize and reward those who stay in step, which will advance them in their chosen careers.

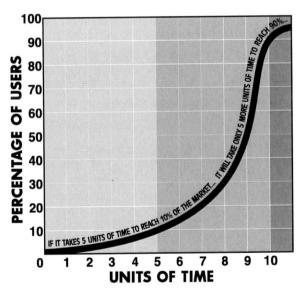

With ideal market penetration, whatever time it takes for a new technology to be accepted by 10 percent of the population, in that same amount of time again, the technology would gain accceptance in up to 90 percent of the population.[3]

Time is money. Access to information is money. Increasingly sophisticated technology will continue to deliver information faster. Anticipate faster, more frequent changes due to more efficient use of technology. And if you haven't already, take a class in computers. Become skilled at using digital tools.

But, at the same time, understand the value of combining "high touch" people skills with your "high tech" computer skills. Being people smart pays big dividends, so seek ways to use the information you discover through *Career Direct*.® In Bill Gates's words, "Analytical [computer] software enables you to shift human resources from data collection to value-added customer service and support where the human touch makes a profound difference."[4]

6. HOME-BASED BUSINESSES MORE POPULAR

More and more, workers who are laid off choose to start their own businesses. Home-based business is now the fastest growing sector of the economy as people try to take advantage of trends that permit greater flexibility and control of time and income.

Depending on the type, starting your own home business may require substantial financial and time resources. Be sure your family is braced for the adjustment. A survey of first-year business owners revealed that half worked between 50 and 70 hours a week; another 25 percent worked more than 70 hours. Only 13 percent of new business owners worked between 40 and 49 hours in running their ventures.[5] Those who want to own a business often discover their business owns them.

7. TELECOMMUTING FROM HOME

With more workers being empowered to make decisions and work independently on projects, a home office with a PC and Internet access is all that is needed for many to telecommute. According to the Bureau of Labor Statistics, in 2004 about 20.7 million people were working at least once a week from home.

The trend will continue for a time, but watch for it to level off. Humans are incredibly social creatures and many will crave the dynamics of the office. Some home workers have expressed shock over suddenly discovering the absence of support services that are available at the office but not at their home: administrative support, brainstorming sessions, copy and fax machines.

8. PREPARATION FOR WORK IS ESSENTIAL

U.S. Department of Labor statistics tell the story of how important a college education is for future earnings, as reported in the Bureau of Labor Statistics' *Current Population Survey*:[6]

Average 2008 Annual Salaries

- No high school diploma - $22,620
- High school graduate - $31,980
- Bachelor's degree - $52,624
- Advanced degree - $65,468

But not all degrees are equally valuable to employers.

Average salaries by occupation:

- Chemical engineer - $84,420
- Computer systems analyst - $75,890
- Sociologist - $67,330
- Historian - $54,630
- Elementary school teacher - $50,040[7]

Note that chemical engineers were valued much higher, by salary, than historians and school teachers.

According to *Careers 2000*, a career-planning publication, "If you want to pursue a business career as such, in industry, finances or health care, the new paradigm says, learn all you can about the world first and pick up the specifics as you go along." Generally speaking, the demand for 21st-century workers is for generalists who have specialist capabilities; a college degree provides broad equipping for work. The article suggests that with so many middle managers eliminated by corporate downsizing in the last decade, there will be a need for generalists who "have core skills that you can leverage throughout the organization, innate qualities of problem solving, leadership, adaptability for change."

However, please be advised: A college degree is no guarantee of a good job. In fact, many current college graduates take jobs that don't require college degrees. And some expect the ratio to climb to one in every four college graduates in the next decade.

Two categories of workers earn substantial income without a college degree. One is entrepreneurs who start their own business. A survey of highly successful U.S. entrepreneurs indicates that only 46 percent received their college degrees; 29 percent never went to college, and 27 percent started college but never finished.[8]

A second category is skilled trades. Many learn a skilled trade in a vocational-technical school setting and make a fine living as cosmetologists, electricians, automotive specialists, heating and air conditioning work, etc.

Unless you're a highly driven entrepreneur or plan to learn a skilled trade in vocational-technical school, getting your college degree should be in your plans. And your education won't stop there. Be prepared to be a lifelong learner by upgrading your skills and knowledge in continuing education classes and seminars.

9. TEMPORARIES AND PART-TIMERS INCREASE

Once regarded as second-class job opportunities, temporaries and part-timers are emerging as respectable, even desirable, career steps. Some highly skilled workers work as temps in order to control their schedules and make time for other priorities. Many companies use temporaries for high-tech work so they can expand their workforce according to workload. Other companies use temporary agencies as a way to screen workers for potentially permanent positions.

Some managers are hired back as consultants by the companies that laid them off. Such contract executives are typically very task-oriented and focused; as a result, they may be contracted at a higher rate of pay than those who survived the cutbacks. Although they are not likely to retain the benefits package of regular employees, their pay scale may make up for the difference.

In deference to stockholder dividends, some corporate cutbacks have gone too deep or been made in the wrong areas, leaving some departments understaffed. We know of companies that offered early retirement packages to some of their employees and then turned around and hired them back as higher-paid contract workers.

Managers are not the only people working temporary positions. Part-time jobs (less than 30 hours a week) are growing, saving employers the thousands of dollars in health benefits paid for a full-time employee. Additional savings for the employer can be found by eliminating vacation time, sick leave, holidays, and retirement benefits for part-timers. A result of this strategy is that more and more American workers are holding down two or three jobs.

10. LIFELONG EDUCATION AND UPGRADING OF SKILLS

Assuming that your current skills are sufficient for tomorrow's workplace is likely to be an exercise in self-delusion. It may have worked in the past, but now that attitude is like sitting in a pit stop during the Indianapolis 500 while the rest of the field races by.

Twenty-first century workers must constantly upgrade and refine their skills, both to compete and to be good stewards of the natural strengths and talents God has given them.

In Matthew 25:14-30, Jesus taught the parable of the talents, understood as a measure of silver in the New Testament. Even though He was speaking of money, the principle applies to the natural talents He has given us. He blesses us when we invest and use them for His glory. In fact, Jesus said, *"To everyone who has, more shall be given, and he will have an abundance; but from the one who does not have, even what he does have shall be taken away"* (Matthew 25:29).

Another way of stating this principle is "use it or lose it." Exercise and develop your talents or they will lose their value.

As followers of Christ, we should anticipate changes in the future workplace with faith and courage. Although it is impossible for us to predict precise details, we know the One who is already there. *"He will not allow your foot to slip; He who keeps you will not slumber"* (Psalm 121:3).

Because we live in an imperfect world, you cannot expect a career pathway that is easy or painless, but God's promise is that you will not walk it alone. He's with you each step of the way.

Corporation to Coach
Ken Gossage goes back to school

Ken Gossage had a lot at stake. Educated as an engineer, he'd worked 17 years for the same company. He'd spent the last seven of those years as manager of a manufacturing/distribution plant. Now, his employer, a medium-sized private company, was being swallowed by a big fish—a public corporation that was 10 times larger. To preserve the gains he'd made, he had to impress his new bosses.

Although Ken had grown frustrated with the corporate world, it had provided his family with a comfortable lifestyle. But as a Christian, he knew that God sometimes makes drastic changes in the lives of His children to shake them out of their comfort zones and move them to total dependence on Him.

Ken and his wife, Dede, began praying, and some friends from Crown in their hometown of Gainesville, Georgia, introduced them to the ministry's *Career Direct*® assessment. "I had planned my own career path in college without considering that God had designed me for His purposes and might have a more fulfilling career in mind," Ken says.

"Interestingly, the best match recommended by the assessment was to teach high school and coach."

Ken had enjoyed coaching when his children were younger, but the obstacle of living off a teacher's salary seemed too great for him to overcome. So, for the next three years he threw himself into his job.

Changes at work

"Trying to impress the new leadership and prove I was where God wanted me to be, I became entangled in the bureaucracy and politics of the giant corporation," he says.

But as Ken worked harder, he seemed to have less influence on the people and decisions around him. Disillusioned and exhausted, he had to make sense of his life, so he asked God for answers.

At this point, some unexplainable events and opportunities came along. "They were not all positive," Ken says, "but through my renewed eyes of faith, they had the unmistakable imprint of God."

On the negative side, Ken's vice president, to whom he had reported since he joined the company fresh out of college, was fired. The VP had worked for the company 25 years.

On the positive side, Ken received some unsolicited information about a unique teacher certification program. Then, a complete stranger to Ken's division of the company was hired to replace his former VP. Within a few months, the new boss shook up the management structure so much that Ken was left with a nice salary but very little responsibility.

"I sensed that God was trying to literally push me out the door," he says. "He had tried discouragement and weariness, and now, on top of all that, boredom. Remembering the counsel I had received from the assessment, I took a small step of faith and applied to the master's degree/certification program that had mysteriously appeared in the mail."

During the next few months, it seemed that each step of faith resulted in an open door for Ken. He was one of 10 people accepted into the very selective certification program. And with his undergraduate engineering degree, he would need only 48 hours (four semesters) to graduate.

Next, he had to unveil his education plan to his new boss and seek that person's approval, which seemed impossible. Instead, the boss replied, "No problem. You let me know what hours you'll work each semester, and when you need to leave permanently, we'll start you on severance pay for six months." Still, Ken and Dede had to wrestle with the issue of how they would live on a teacher's salary, and the following months were stressful for both of them as they considered future expenses like college for two teenage children.

Changes at home

In an effort to avoid conflict with Dede, Ken had limited communication with her about his plans. "If I could do it all over again, I would discuss my plans with her," he says. "Husbands and wives are supposed to be one. A man needs the support of his wife, and she needs to know what he's doing."

With the burden of working 35 to 40 hours per week and spending 15 hours per week in school, Ken needed help from somewhere, and he spent much of his free time talking to the Lord and getting assurance from Him.

When Ken first shared his education plans with Dede, her initial reaction was that "he should go and pray about it some more." She was a stay-at-home mom and had a part-time business, which allowed her a lot of flexibility. If Ken became a teacher, she knew her lifestyle would have to change. In the months that followed, both of them came to a place of brokenness, but Dede was confident that, in time, they would work it out. "I think God wanted to teach us a new level of trust," she says. "I probably suffered from a 'rights' mentality. I laid that down and forced myself to do things for Ken that I knew he would appreciate. This added to the healing process."

Dede worked part-time as an interior decorator, and when Ken got a teaching job, she and her daughter, Daphne, decorated his class. This allowed her to be a part of his world. She also attended his high school football games, even though she had never been a football fan. "It's a lot of fun," she says, "especially when you're winning."

A change for the better

Ken left the company where he had been employed 20 years and began student teaching in January 2000. He drew his severance pay, which expired exactly when he received his first paycheck as a teacher. In July 2003, Ken's former employer announced that in September it would close the plant he had managed.

As a math teacher, Ken was in high demand and received several teaching offers, but he was drawn to a small public school in Buford, Georgia.

His coaching duties at Buford include football and junior varsity baseball, and in the three years he has been at the school, the football team has played in three state championship games.

It has won the state championship the last two years and had a winning streak of 30 straight games going into the fall 2003 season.

"During my first three years, I have experienced what most coaches or teachers never experience in a lifetime," Ken says. "Now that's a rewarding job!"

Since Ken's successes as a teacher and coach, God has provided the latest step in his career journey—as the headmaster of a local Christian school. With each step, Ken is learning more about God's plan and purpose for his life. ■

Your Response

So what do I do now?

Write at least one Action Step in response to the chapter you have just read. If you write more than one, prioritize them in a logical order so you have a clear first step that you can begin immediately.

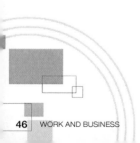

Action Steps _____

_____

_____

_____

_____

_____

_____

We also encourage you to reward yourself for every Action Step completed. Since the enemy ("the accuser") will discourage you by making the journey seem impossibly long, you need to see each step as its own victory. Your progress will be faster and more enjoyable if you take a little time to celebrate it.

Your celebration doesn't have to take a lot of time or money to be meaningful. Just make it something you enjoy, and tie it to the Action Step you have completed.

Celebration Plan _____

_____

_____

_____

_____

_____

_____

ENDNOTES

1. North American Free Trade Agreement.

2. General Agreement on Tariffs and Trade.

3. "S-curves are frequently used to estimate or forecast the rate of adoption of a technology, the rate at which the performance of a technology improves, or the market penetration of a technology or product over time. Implicit in S-curve forecasting are assumptions of slow initial growth, subsequent rapid growth, followed by declining growth as saturation levels are achieved," says Stephen R. Lawrence, Associate Professor of Operations Management at The College of Business and Administration, University of Colorado at Boulder. His practical worksheet and demonstration of S-curve theory can be found at http://www-bus.colorado.edu/faculty/lawrence/TOOLS/SCurve/scurve.xls.

4. Bill Gates, *Business @ the Speed of Thought*. New York: Warner Books, 1999, p. 235.

5. Norman M. Scarbrough and Thomas W. Zimmerer, "Entrepreneurs: The Driving Force Behind Small Business," *Effective Small Business Management* (NY: MacMillan), Fourth Edition, p. 4.

6. U.S. Department of Labor, Bureau of Labor Statistics, *Current Population Survey*, Quarter 1, 2008.

7. U.S. Department of Labor, Bureau of Labor Statistics, *Occupational Employment and Wages*, May 2007.

8. A. Gary Shilling, "Cutting Deals," *Forbes*, January 30, 1995, p. 142.

CHAPTER 2

STARTING A BUSINESS

Many people consider going into business for themselves, and sometimes it is a good option. Starting a business can be a complex undertaking, requiring much prayer and consideration, and we could not begin to cover every aspect in this brief book.

Crown Financial Ministries has learned a lot from counseling with people who have started businesses—some successfully and others not. In this chapter we will highlight key areas and ask questions to help you evaluate the wisdom of starting your own business.

Motivation

As in most other decisions, you should always analyze your motivation for pursuing a course of action. Proper motivation for starting a business might include a strong desire to provide a product or service or a specific talent that could be marketed by you better than by someone else. Among the strongest motivations are flexibility and care of a family member. Among the drawbacks are never getting away from work and interference with family life. There is a delicate balance between owning a business and having a business that owns you. Quite often people want to start a business out of frustration with their current employment situation. That may or may not be a good idea since, for most people, there are other alternatives. The following questions will help you analyze your motivations.

What is your real motivation for considering self-employment?

List your reasons in order of priority.

(1) _____

(2) _____

(3) _____

(4) _____

(5) _____

What don't you like about your current situation?

What options have you considered other than self-employment?

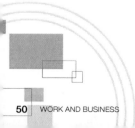

What values and needs are not being met in your current situation?

Starting a business requires commitment and hard work. It can be a challenge of enormous magnitude, and it usually takes a burning desire to overcome the obstacles.

Is this something you really want and feel strongly led to do?

Knowledge/Experience

Larry Burkett often advised not getting financially involved in things we don't know much about. That principle especially applies to starting a business with its required investment of money, time and energy.

What is your knowledge level about the business you would undertake?

Do you know what defines a Christian business, and have you studied God's principles for operating a business?

Note: Check Crown's *Business by the Book Independent Study* with workbook and DVD video for additional study.

How much actual hands-on experience do you have in the occupational field you are considering?

Do you have any business experience (profit and loss responsibility)?

Have you investigated government regulations concerning the potential business? Are professional licenses or registrations required?

Are you knowledgeable about the income and Social Security tax requirements that govern self-employed individuals?

NOTE: This can be a shock to those who have not had to pay quarterly taxes or self-employment tax.

Do you know how to write a business plan? Have you written a business plan?

Note: If not, check with the Small Business Development Center near you, or investigate computer software programs designed to help you write your business plan.

"He who tills his land will have plenty of food, but he who follows empty pursuits will have poverty in plenty" (Proverbs 28:19).

Startup Capital

Most businesses fail in the first two years because they are undercapitalized. Before launching into a business, you need to count the cost of everything you will need to succeed.

Rather than be too optimistic, plan conservatively regarding income and liberally regarding expenses. A frequent problem in young businesses is not generating adequate income to pay overhead and provide a livable income. Entrepreneurs tend to be too optimistic about how long it will take to reach and sustain profitability. They end up living off money that should be paying the overhead (creditors), and they sink further in debt while trying to hold on until the business takes off.

During business startup, many people make the mistake of paying living expenses by using a line of credit or credit cards. This piling up of debt virtually guarantees a financial disaster and should be avoided.

Where will your startup and operating capital come from?

Do you have enough cash or liquid assets to operate 18 months to two years without a profit? (That's how long it takes for most successful businesses to become profitable. The unsuccessful ones never do.)

Are you considering forming a partnership?

NOTE: Experience shows that partnerships seldom work out. If you are yoked to someone whose personal (including spouse) values and motivations differ from yours, you won't be very happy. It's similar to a marriage, except more difficult to maintain. Successful partnerships require both parties to have the mind of Christ (a servant's attitude toward the other partner). With two or more families involved, this rarely occurs.

Keeping Financial Records

Those who have an entrepreneurial bent rarely enjoy detail work, such as record keeping.

Not having good financial records can cause major problems, because a business owner must make decisions every day based on current financial realities and trends. If you don't know where you stand financially, you run a high risk of acting in ignorance and making a bad, costly decision.

Keep in mind that the best record-keeping system for you will be something you can thoroughly understand. You may have to get some help at first and do some study on your own as well, but the keys to remember are simplicity and timeliness. Having something that is simple and current is essential for sound financial management.

What plans have you made for keeping simple, timely, and accurate financial records?

Who will be the detail person in your operation? Can you do it? Will your spouse be better suited to this task? Or will you hire someone to assist you?

If you are not experienced with financial records, such as income statements, balance statements, and budgets, how will you become knowledgeable about them?

"Listen to counsel and accept discipline, that you may be wise the rest of your days" (Proverbs 19:20).

Counsel and Information

You'll need information from several sources, but your counsel should come from those who have a godly perspective toward everything in life. Local Christian businesspeople can be your best source of counsel.

Small Business Development Centers, operated through state universities, are located in most states. They provide help to people who are considering business startups and to those who already own businesses. Information is usually free or provided at low cost.

Have you sought and received adequate counsel regarding the pros and cons of owning your own business?

Have you developed a list of sources for counsel and information?

Personnel

The simplest business by far is a one-person operation in which the owner is the business. However, many situations will require additional employees. The minute you hire one person, many laws and rules apply that complicate the workload. You need to be familiar with withholding taxes, Social Security taxes (FICA), the Fair Labor Employment Act, Occupational Safety and Health Administration (OSHA) regulations, Worker's Compensation, and many other areas. Also, in any business, hiring the right people is crucially important.

A bad hire is one of the worst things that can happen to a small business owner. Develop a job description and criteria for the job before you start looking for the person. Understand your personality's weaknesses in order to find employees whose strengths complement them.

"The body is not one member, but many" (1 Corinthians 12:14).

As you look for personnel, keep in mind the principles you have learned earlier in this book about matching the person to the job. The same concepts apply. If you know the pattern needed to do the job, you can look for a person with that pattern when hiring. Generally, we find that an entrepreneur's first hire should be someone with opposing strengths. If you are a big-picture person, you will likely need a detailed person to follow through on day-to-day activities and record keeping. Conversely, if you are a detailed person, you will likely need an outgoing, enterprising person to promote the business.

You should seriously consider obtaining a *Career Direct*® assessment for any prospective employee. Consider the following questions before hiring someone.

Are you familiar with the rules and regulations that apply to employees?

Have you developed a written job description for the opening you want to fill?

Have you given consideration to the pattern of the person you want to hire?

Skills and Abilities _____

Vocational Interests _____

Work Values _____

Personality Style _____

Timing a Business Startup

As in any other endeavor, timing can be of the utmost importance—timing that applies to you in your life and situation as well as timing that applies to the product and services you offer.

Is the endeavor compatible with your life and other responsibilities at this time?

Has the window of opportunity closed, just opened, or not be open until some future date?

Is the timing right for this particular product or service?

This is really a marketing question that will require some careful thought, advice, and research.

"The way of a fool is right in his own eyes, but a wise man is he who listens to counsel" (Proverbs 12:15). *"The sluggard is wiser in his own eyes than seven men who can give a discreet answer"* (Proverbs 26:16).

Personality

Generally, entrepreneurs tend to operate with a personality style that is confident, results-oriented, problem-solving, and challenge-oriented (Dominant type). They are usually big-picture visionaries who believe they can overcome any obstacles that arise. There are, however, good examples of every personality style being effective as business leaders.

The secret is to know your areas of strength and struggles and arrange the majority of your work load to fall within your strengths.

You can adapt as necessary to accomplish work in your weaker areas, but you should be aware that any time you adapt very much for an extended period of time, stress results. If you have high needs for stability and security, you may not want to undertake the risks of being an entrepreneur. At the very least, you need to understand how people with your personality style recharge after stressful work outside their areas of strength.

Entrepreneurs generally must be willing to take risks; sometimes they succeed and sometimes they fail. The principle of risk versus return applies the same way here as in any other investment. The higher the anticipated return, the higher the risk. You should understand your personality style, along with your tolerance for risk, and give this area high priority in your decision to start a business.

Is your temperament suited to owning and operating your own business? Evaluate your strengths based on the information in the results of your *Career Direct® Complete Guidance System* report and the entrepreneur appraisal below.

ENTREPRENEUR APPRAISAL

Assess your personal potential to operate your own home-based business. Circle a number for each statement to indicate how well it describes you or how you feel:

1=not at all
2=sometimes
3=often
4=usually
5=always

1 2 3 4 5   I like to be in charge and usually lead groups in which I work.

1 2 3 4 5   I tend to see the whole picture and all aspects of any project.

1 2 3 4 5   I am a leader of people; others look to me for direction.

1 2 3 4 5   I realistically assess my talents and abilities.

1 2 3 4 5   I ask for advice from experts in fields in which I need help.

1 2 3 4 5   I am thorough and I accurately complete the tasks I begin.

1 2 3 4 5   I enjoy solving problems and see obstacles as opportunities.

1 2 3 4 5   I schedule my day and my activities and stick to my schedule.

1 2 3 4 5   Taking risks gives me a feeling of excitement.

1 2 3 4 5   I delegate work to others, remove myself from the project, and
            accept their processes and results.

1 2 3 4 5   I usually bounce back very quickly after a setback.

1 2 3 4 5   I am willing to devote myself to my business.

1 2 3 4 5   My attention is not easily diverted from tasks.

1 2 3 4 5   I have a planned budget that I do not exceed.

1 2 3 4 5   I don't usually buy from door-to-door or telephone solicitors.

1 2 3 4 5   I accept responsibility for the outcome of projects I undertake.

1 2 3 4 5   Disappointments and delays do not deter me from plans or
            goals I have set for myself.

1 2 3 4 5   I am goal-oriented and have a 1-year, 5-year, and 10-year plan.

1 2 3 4 5   I balance my checkbook every month.

1 2 3 4 5   After much prayer, I feel strongly that God is leading me in the
            home-based business direction.

"No servant can serve two masters; for either he will hate the one and love the other, or else he will be devoted to one and despise the other. You cannot serve God and wealth" (Luke 16:13).

Time - Energy - Family

A realistic evaluation of the time commitment required to start and operate a business is essential. Solving one problem after another will require energy—physical energy and emotional energy—that comes from your drive and enthusiasm to see a project completed. Counting the cost is important, because we know three things that are true about pursuing success at any level:

1. The price you pay to succeed is intensely personal—it is not the same for any two people.

2. The price is always costly; worthwhile things never come without investment of time and resources.

3. The price is not negotiable; either you do what is required or you don't. You can't barter with true success.

So, a business startup can be an all-consuming experience, and frequently marriages and families suffer, even to the point of breakup. Consider these questions in this area.

Do you understand the time commitment required to see this undertaking through successfully?

Are you a high-energy person? Is your enthusiasm so high or motivation so great that your work will seem like play?

How will the business affect your relationship with your spouse?

How will the business affect your relationship with your children? Will you be able to spend quantity time as well as quality time with your family?

How will your business endeavors affect your relationship with the Lord?

"Whatever you do, do your work heartily, as for the Lord rather than for men" (Colossians 3:23).

God's Will

Go back to the first section on motivation in this chapter. Consider your true motivations for pursuing this course of action in light of what you believe God wants you to do.

Have you diligently sought God's will in this decision?

Will this decision enable you to better glorify the Lord in your work?

Do you and your spouse both have peace in the decision that this is God's will for your life?

If you are single, have you received confirmation from a parent or other Christian mentor?

Conclusion

We have taken you through the above issues because they cover the "Hall of Horrors" museum of common mistakes made when starting a business. It is not intended to discourage you but to assist you in making a good decision.

Remember, every situation is different, so every issue won't apply with the same significance. If you are going to sell homemade pies to your friends and neighbors, your situation is fairly simple, but if you expand into a small baking operation that employs several people, your situation will be much more complex.

We can't emphasize enough the importance of prayerful and patient consideration when making a decision to start a business. If you are committed to doing God's will in your life, you can experience the advantage of being in business for yourself, but not by yourself. The Lord will supply His wisdom when you ask with a motivation to serve Him humbly. Do your homework and let the Lord guide you into His will.

Radical Transformation
Ken Atkins

Ken Atkins is a sixth generation Floridian. His dad was a successful dentist, and his grandfather, a mechanical engineer, was among three scientists who patented the process for making frozen orange juice concentrate.

Growing up in Winter Haven, Florida, Ken was blessed—from a material standpoint. His family had a nice home, new cars, properties, and horses.

They celebrated Thanksgiving and Christmas and prayed before meals, but Ken wasn't brought up in church. In fact, he learned to be wary of churches, believing that they were places where fanatics and hypocrites congregated.

A career, a house, a lot of debt

Following in his grandfather's footsteps, Ken decided to become an engineer. He earned an ROTC scholarship that paid for his first four years of higher education.

As a senior, he was called out of college to attend officer training school during Operation Desert Storm. But after Iraq quickly succumbed to the U.S. and other allied forces, his officer training class was the first that didn't have to go to the Middle East.

He entered the Army Reserves in 1990 and went on to earn a master's degree in engineering. He left active Reserve duty in 2003.

"After Desert Storm, I started to work

as a civil engineer in Orlando," says Ken, who married his wife, Maria, at age 20.

He remembers Larry Burkett saying that some young couples look at their parents' possessions and forget that those possessions were accumulated over many years. These couples try to match what their parents own in less than five years, which results in tremendous debt.

"I tried to obtain everything my family had, and it caused a lot of problems," Ken says. "Maria and I both had new cars, we bought a house, and we bought everything to furnish the house. We lived in downtown Orlando in an old home, and when we moved in, everything broke." Almost overnight, the couple had accumulated a mortgage, family loans, and $55,000 in additional debt.

Far away from God

In addition, Maria, who had grown up in church, stopped attending church after she met Ken.

"I led her away rather than her leading me toward Christ," he says. "I didn't want anything to do with the church. I felt that it was bondage and that it was people telling me how to run my life, which is what I had been taught."

Ken was hired by a university to teach engineering in the evenings, and during his drive to work, he began listening to J. Vernon McGee's "Through the Bible" radio program.

"He happened to be talking about Vietnam vets, which kind of interested me, being a lieutenant in the Reserves at the time," Ken says. "Then, I came across Larry Burkett and his program. I really didn't care for the Christian content, but I knew Larry had worked with NASA, and that interested me. He was down to earth and completely different from some of the showy televangelists I had seen while flipping through channels on the television."

During this time, Ken was carrying about 12 credit cards and shifting the balance from one card to another in order to stay ahead. But his debt grew harder and harder to manage.

About one year later, Ken's platoon went on a two-week training exercise. As a lieutenant, he was in the command center, where he had access to a radio that allowed him to hear 14 straight days of Larry Burkett broadcasts. At the end of that time, he accepted Christ as his Savior.

A financial wake-up call

While he was in the field, Ken contracted an illness that he believes was malaria. He suffered from a 103-degree fever for several days, and during this time, he dreamed that he died.

He could see his wife struggling with the financial problems he had left behind. When his fever finally broke and he was able to get back on his feet, he began taking action to change his financial situation.

He and Maria began tithing, attending First Baptist in Orlando, and growing in their faith. "I read everything there was to read that Larry had ever published and just became a real fan of his ministry and began to support it," Ken says.

Based on advice he received from the ministry, Ken contacted Consumer

Credit Counseling Service and began
paying off his debt.

"In four years we paid off all the $55,000
we owed," he says. "I was making a base
engineer's salary, which was not enough to
pay off the debt in four years. But God blessed
us in enormous ways. We got income tax refunds we
weren't expecting, checks from title companies and insurance
companies, and dividend checks."

Growing in knowledge

Like many people who've benefited from God's financial
principles, Ken wanted to help others. He completed Crown's
Money Map Coach training course and one of the ministry's
life group financial studies.

After reading the testimony of Ken Gossage (see page 42) in a
Crown publication, he also went through the ministry's *Career
Direct*® assessment with his business partner, Jonathon Bray.

Blessings at work and at home

Based on principles from Larry Burkett's *Business by the
Book*, Ken and Jonathon started their own engineering company.

Other people told them that their company would not succeed
if they kept their commitment to:

- give 10 percent of their gross business income to the
  Lord's work and

- close at least half a day on Thursdays in order to volun-
  teer for Crown.

At first, the company had a single client who built one home per year. Within a couple of months, it had about 15 clients, and within one year it was debt free. Last year the company grossed $300,000, and Ken and Jonathon were able to give $30,000 to God's work.

However, Ken's blessings have gone far beyond the financial realm. During his and Maria's 15-year marriage, they had been unable to have children. They adopted three children ages 6, 5, and 4.

"We were not supposed to be able to have children," Ken says. "They told us there was no chance, but my wife just delivered a baby. And, our other three children are glad to have another sibling.

"Without Crown, I know I wouldn't be where I am today. I read Crown materials in my spare time, and I think I've just about read everything the ministry has produced. Jonathon and I even have a Crown library in our office. So, without doubt, Larry Burkett and Howard Dayton's ministry has really changed my life, and it continues to do so." ■

Your Response

Action Steps _____

_____

_____

_____

_____

_____

_____

_____

_____

Celebration Plan _____

_____

_____

_____

_____

_____

_____

_____

CHAPTER 3

WRAPPING IT UP WITH HOPE

All Honest Professions Are Honorable

Scripture gives dignity to all types of work, not elevating any honest profession above another. David was a shepherd and a king. Luke was a doctor. Lydia was a retailer of purple fabric. Daniel was a government worker. Paul was a tentmaker. And, finally, the Lord Jesus was a carpenter.

In God's economy, there is equal dignity in the labor of the automobile mechanic and the president of General Motors, in the labor of the pastor and a secretary serving the church.

God Is Involved with You in Your Work

We have already established that work is not a curse but rather one of God's gifts to you. It is a gift that develops your aptitudes, your character, and gives you dignity. It also facilitates your service and influence because, regardless of where you work, you are "ambassadors for Christ" (2 Corinthians 5:20).

God has not given you the responsibility of work and then left you to sink or swim on your own. He continues to be involved with you in several ways.

1. God gives job skills.

Exodus 36:1 illustrates this truth: *"Every skillful person in whom the Lord has put skill and understanding to know how to perform all the work . . . shall perform."* God has given you unique aptitudes. People have a wide variety of abilities, manual skills, and intellectual capacities. This does not imply that one person is better than another, merely that each has received a unique set of abilities.

2. God gives success.

The life of Joseph is a perfect example of God helping a person to succeed. *"The Lord was with Joseph, so he became a successful man. . . . His master saw that the Lord was with him and how the Lord caused all that he did to prosper"* (Genesis 39:2-3). Although you have certain responsibilities, it is ultimately God who gives success.

3. God controls promotion.

Psalm 75:6-7 says, *"For promotion and power come from nowhere on earth, but only from God"* (TLB). As much as it may surprise you, your boss is not the one who controls whether you will be promoted. Don't make the mistake of leaving God out of your work, believing that you alone are responsible for your abilities and success; that is a formula for stress and frustration. Consider this question: If

God gives you your abilities and controls success and promotion, how should this affect your work?

You Have a Career Edge

As a follower of Christ, God's Spirit within you is transforming you into a person with character qualities that any employer would value. Daniel (of lion's den fame) is a great example of a model employee.

The sixth chapter of Daniel shows Darius, the king of Babylon, appointing 120 people to administer the government, and three people—one of whom was Daniel—to supervise the administrators. Because of Daniel's outstanding service, King Darius later decided to promote Daniel to govern the entire kingdom.

Daniel's jealous peers looked for a way to disqualify him but could find no basis for accusation. Knowing Daniel's devotion to God, they asked King Darius to enact a law requiring everyone to worship only the king or die in the lion's den. Daniel refused to stop worshipping God, and Darius reluctantly threw him to the lions. When God rescued Daniel by sending an angel to shut the lions' mouths, the overjoyed king ordered all of his subjects to fear and reverence the God of Daniel.

Consider six character qualities exhibited by Daniel.

1. Honesty

Daniel 6:4 tells us that Daniel's fellow employees could find no dishonesty in him, and there was no "evidence of corruption" in his work. Daniel was an example of total honesty, a crucial character quality in the work-place as well as in the rest of life.

2. Faithfulness

"He was faithful" (Daniel 6:4). You will exhibit growing faithfulness and excellence in your work as you whole-heartedly serve God and become more like Him.

3. Prayerfulness

Godly employees are people of prayer. *"When Daniel knew that the document was signed [restricting worship to the king alone] . . . he continued kneeling on his knees three times a day, praying and giving thanks before his God, as he had been doing previously"* (Daniel 6:10). Daniel shouldered the responsibility of governing the most powerful country of his day. Few of us will ever face that kind of pressure or demands on our time. Yet he knew the importance of prayer. If you are not praying consistently, your work is suffering.

4. Loyalty—Honors Employer

"Daniel spoke to the king, 'O king, live forever!'" (Daniel 6:21). After surviving the deceived king's sentence, Daniel could have responded in many disrespect-ful ways, including threatening the king with God's judgment. Instead, he remained loyal, honoring his employer with both his words and his work.

Godly employees always honor their supe-riors. *"Servants [employees], be submis-sive to your masters [employers] with all respect, not only to those who are good*

and gentle, but also to those who are unreasonable" (1 Peter 2:18). One way we honor employers is refusing to gossip or belittle them behind their back regardless of their weaknesses.

5. Humility—Honors Fellow Employees

People may damage your reputation or attempt to have you fired from your job to secure a promotion over you. Not only did they do that to Daniel, they even tried to murder him in the process. Despite this, there is no evidence that he did anything but honor his fellow employees. His humility recognized that God was both his judge and defense, and that he did not need to resort to the tactics that had been used against him. *"Do not slander a servant [employee] to his master [employer], or he will curse you"* (Proverbs 30:10, NIV).

Godly employees avoid office politics and manipulation to secure a promotion. Your boss does not control your promotion; God Himself does. You can be content in your job as you focus on being faithful, honoring superiors, and encouraging other employees. Having done this, you can rest, knowing that Christ will promote you if and when He chooses.

6. Boldness—Verbalizes Faith

This sixth character quality of Daniel belongs in a slightly different category. Any employer is likely to value the first five qualities as being directly beneficial to your work performance. Boldness may be considered that way as well, although when it comes to your faith, employers will vary considerably in their response.

This is not to suggest keeping quiet about your faith. On the contrary, we suggest a boldness that is gracious and backed by the strength of the first five qualities. What really sets this sixth quality apart is that it represents a big-picture view of your role in the workplace. God has positioned you where He has for reasons that transcend providing your salary. As His ambassador, you represent Him to those around you.

King Darius would never have known about God if Daniel had not communicated his faith at appropriate moments while at work. *"The king spoke and said to Daniel, 'Daniel, servant of the living God, has your God, whom you constantly serve, been able to deliver you from the lions?'"* (Daniel 6:20).

Daniel's words and actions worked in tandem to influence King Darius, who observed his honesty, faithfulness, and hard work. Listen to the king's response: *"I issue a decree that in every part of my kingdom people must fear and reverence the God of Daniel. For He is the living God and He endures forever"* (Daniel 6:26, NIV).

Daniel influenced his employer, one of the most powerful people in the world, to believe in the only true God. You have that same opportunity in your God-given sphere of work. A job well done earns you the right to tell others with whom you work about the reality of Christ. Viewing your work from God's

perspective turns dissatisfaction to contentment with a job well done; drudgery becomes excitement over the prospect of introducing others to the Savior.

Your Response

Action Steps _____

_____

_____

_____

_____

_____

_____

_____

_____

_____

Celebration Plan _____

_____

_____

_____

_____

_____

_____

_____

INTRODUCTION TO CHRIST

As important as our financial welfare is, it is not our highest priority. The single most important need of every person everywhere is to know God and experience the gift of His forgiveness and peace.

These five biblical truths will show you God's open door through a personal relationship with Jesus Christ.

1. God loves you and wants you to know Him and experience a meaningful life.

God created people in His own image, and He desires a close relationship with each of us. *"For God so loved the world, that He gave His only begotten Son, that whoever believes in Him shall not perish, but have eternal life"* (John 3:16). *"I [Jesus] came that they might have life, and have it abundantly"* (John 10:10).

God the Father loved you so much that He gave His only Son, Jesus Christ, to die for you.

2. Unfortunately, we are separated from God.

Because God is holy and perfect, no sin can abide in His presence. Every person has sinned, and the consequence of sin is separation from God. *"All have sinned and fall short of the glory of God"* (Romans 3:23). *"Your sins have cut you off from God"* (Isaiah 59:2, TLB).

3. God's only provision to bridge this gap is Jesus Christ.

Jesus Christ died on the cross to pay the penalty for our sin, bridging the gap between God and us. Jesus said, *"I am the way, and the truth, and the life; no one comes to the Father but through Me"* (John 14:6). *"God demonstrates His own love towards us, in that while we were yet sinners, Christ died for us"* (Romans 5:8).

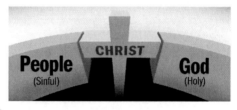

4. This relationship is a gift from God.

Our efforts can never achieve the perfection God requires. The only solution was to provide it to us as a gift.

When Jesus bore our sins on the cross, paying our penalty forever, He exchanged His righteousness for our guilt. By faith, we receive the gift we could never deserve.

Is that fair? Of course not! God's love exceeds His justice, resulting in mercy and grace toward us.

"It is by grace you have been saved, through faith— and this is not from yourselves, it is the gift of God— not by works, so that no one can boast" (Ephesians 2:8-9, NIV).

5. **We must each receive Jesus Christ individually.**

Someone has said that God has no grandchildren. Each of us is responsible before God for our own sin. We can continue to bear the responsibility and pay the consequences or we can receive the gift of Jesus' righteousness, enabling God to declare us "Not guilty!"

If you desire to know the Lord and are not certain whether you have this relationship, we encourage you to receive Christ right now. Pray a prayer similar to this suggested one:

"God, I need You. I invite Jesus to come into my life as my Savior and Lord and to make me the person You want me to be. Thank You for forgiving my sins and for giving me the gift of eternal life."

You may be successful in avoiding financial quicksand—and we pray you will be—but without a relationship with Christ, it won't have lasting value. Eternal perspective begins with Him.

If you ask Christ into your life, please tell some people you know who are also following Christ. They will encourage you and help you get involved in a Bible-teaching church where you can grow spiritually. And please let us know as well. We would love to help in any way we can.

GOD'S OWNERSHIP & FINANCIAL FAITHFULNESS

How we view God determines how we live. Viewing Him as Savior is a good beginning, but growth comes when we view Him as Lord.

After losing his children and all his possessions, Job continued to worship God because he knew God was the Lord of those possessions and retained the ultimate rights over them. Realizing that God owed him nothing and he owed God everything enabled him to submit to God's authority and find contentment.

Moses walked away from his earthly inheritance, regarding *"disgrace for the sake of Christ as of greater value than the treasures of Egypt"* because he had his eye on God's reward (Hebrews 11:26, NIV).

Our willingness, like theirs, to give up a lesser value for a greater one, requires recognizing what most of the world does not: God is not only the Creator and Owner of all but also the ultimate definer of value. Those responsibilities belong to Him. He has retained them because He alone is capable of handling them.

Most of the frustration we experience in handling money comes when we take God's responsibilities on our own shoulders. Successful money management requires us to understand three aspects of God's Lordship—three roles for which He retains responsibility.

1. GOD OWNS IT ALL.

God owns all our possessions. *"To the Lord your God belong . . . the earth and everything in it"* (Deuteronomy 10:14, NIV). *"The earth is the Lord's, and all it contains"* (Psalm 24:1).

Leviticus 25:23 identifies Him as the owner of all the land: *"The land . . . shall not be sold permanently, for the land is Mine."* Haggai 2:8 says that He owns the precious metals: *"'The silver is Mine and the gold is Mine,' declares the Lord of hosts."*

Even our body—the one thing for which we would tend to claim total ownership—is not our own. *"Or do you not know that your body is a temple of the Holy Spirit who is in you, whom you have from God, and that you are not your own?"* (1 Corinthians 6:19).

The Lord created all things, and He never transferred the ownership of His creation to people. In Colossians 1:17 we are told that, *"In Him all things hold together."* At this very moment the Lord holds everything together by His power. As we will see throughout this study, recognizing God's ownership is crucial in allowing Jesus Christ to become the Lord of our money and possessions.

• Yielding Our Ownership to His Lordship

If we are to be genuine followers of Christ, we must transfer ownership of our possessions to Him. *"None of you can be My disciple who does not give up all his own possessions"* (Luke 14:33). Sometimes He tests us by asking us to give up the very possessions that are most important to us.

The most vivid example of this in Scripture is when God instructed Abraham, *"Take now your son, your only son, whom you love, Isaac . . . and offer him there as a burnt offering"* (Genesis 22:2). When Abraham obeyed, demonstrating his willingness to give up his most valuable possession, God responded, *"Do not lay a hand on the boy . . . now I know that you fear God, because you have not withheld from Me your son"* (Genesis 22:12, NIV).

When we acknowledge God's ownership, every spending decision becomes a spiritual decision. No longer do we ask, "Lord, what do You want me to do with my money?" It becomes, "Lord, what do You want me to do with Your money?" When we have this attitude and handle His money according to His wishes, spending and saving decisions become as spiritual as giving decisions.

• Recognizing God's Ownership

Our culture—the media, even the law—says that what you possess, you own. Acknowledging God's ownership requires a transformation of thinking, and this can be difficult. Many people say that God owns it all while they cling desperately to possessions that they think define them.

Here are a number of practical suggestions to help us recognize God's ownership.

- For the next 30 days, meditate on 1 Chronicles 29:11-12 when you first awake and just before going to sleep.

- For the next 30 days, ask God to make you aware of His ownership and help you to be thankful for it.

- Establish the habit of acknowledging God's ownership every time you buy something.

Recognizing God's ownership is important in learning contentment. When you believe you own something, you are more vulnerable to its circumstances. If it suffers loss or damage, your attitude can swing quickly from happy to discontented.

Recognizing it as God's loss doesn't make it irrelevant, but it does change your perspective. Now you can focus on how He will use this incident in causing *"all things to work together for good to those who love God, to those who are called according to His purpose"* (Romans 8:28).

2. GOD CONTROLS IT ALL.

Besides being Creator and Owner, God is ultimately in control of every event that occurs upon the earth. *"We adore*

you as being in control of everything" (1 Chronicles 29:11, TLB).
"Whatever the Lord pleases, He
does, in heaven and in earth" (Psalm
135:6). And in the book of Daniel,
King Nebuchadnezzar stated: "I praised
the Most High; I honored and glorified him
who lives forever. . . . He does as he pleases with
the powers of heaven and the peoples of the earth. No
one can hold back his hand or say to him: 'What have
you done?'" (Daniel 4:34-35, NIV).

God is also in control of difficult events. "I am the Lord,
and there is no other, the One forming light and creating darkness, causing well-being and creating calamity;
I am the Lord who does all these" (Isaiah 45:6-7).

It is important for us to realize that our heavenly Father
uses even seemingly devastating circumstances for
ultimate good in the lives of the godly. "We know that
God causes all things to work together for good to
those who love God, to those who are called according to His purpose" (Romans 8:28). God allows difficult
circumstances for three reasons.

- **He accomplishes His intentions.**

This is illustrated in the life of Joseph, who was sold
into slavery as a teenager by his jealous brothers.
Joseph later said to his brothers: "Do not be distressed
and do not be angry with yourselves for selling me
here, because it was to save lives that God sent me
ahead of you. . . . It was not you who sent me here,
but God. . . . You intended to harm me, but God

intended it for good to accomplish what is now being done, the saving of many lives" (Genesis 45:5, 8; 50:20, NIV).

• He develops our character.

Godly character, something that is precious in His sight, is often developed during trying times. *"We also rejoice in our sufferings, because we know that suffering produces perseverance; perseverance, character"* (Romans 5:3-4, NIV).

• He disciplines His children.

"Those whom the Lord loves He disciplines. . . . He disciplines us for our good, so that we may share His holiness. All discipline for the moment seems not to be joyful, but sorrowful; yet to those who have been trained by it, afterwards it yields the peaceful fruit of righteousness" (Hebrews 12:6,10-11).

When we are disobedient, we can expect our loving Lord to discipline us, often through difficult circumstances. His purpose is to encourage us to abandon our sin and to "share His holiness."

You can be at peace knowing that your loving heavenly Father is in control of every situation you will ever face. He will use every one of them for a good purpose.

3. GOD PROVIDES IT ALL.

God promises to provide our needs. *"But seek first His kingdom and His righteousness, and all these things [food and*

clothing] will be added to you"
(Matthew 6:33).

The same God who fed manna to
the children of Israel during their 40
years of wandering in the wilderness
and who fed 5,000 with only five loaves
and two fish has promised to provide our
needs. This is the same God who told Elijah,
*"I have commanded the ravens to provide for you
there. . . . The ravens brought him bread and meat
in the morning and bread and meat in the evening"*
(1 Kings 17:4, 6).

God—Both Predictable and Unpredictable

God is totally predictable in His faithfulness to provide for our
needs. What we cannot predict is how He will provide. He uses
various and often surprising means—an increase in income or
a gift. He may provide an opportunity to stretch limited resources
through money-saving purchases. Regardless of how He
chooses to provide for our needs, He is completely reliable.

Our culture believes that God plays no part in financial matters; they assume that His invisibility means He is uninvolved.
They try to shoulder responsibilities that God never intended
for them—burdens of ownership, control, and provision that
only He can carry.

Jesus said, *"Come to Me, all who are weary and heavy-laden,
and I will give you rest. Take My yoke upon you. . . . For My
yoke is easy, and My burden is light"* (Matthew 11:28-30). This
is the only way we can rest and enjoy the peace of God.

When we trust God to do His part in our finances, we can focus on doing our part: being financially faithful with every resource He has given us.

Defining Financial Faithfulness

Faithfully living by God's financial principles doesn't necessarily mean having a pile of money in the bank, but it does bring an end to overdue bills and their related stress. And that's not the most important part; that's just relief from symptoms.

Consider some of the big-picture benefits:

- Assurance that God is in control of our circumstances
- Absolute faith in His promise to meet all of our needs
- A clear conscience before God
- A clear conscience with others

This is not to say that we will live on financial autopilot with no more challenges for the rest of our lives. God promises no such thing. In fact, without challenges our faith has no opportunity to be perfected or even to grow; without challenges it isn't active or visible. But peace in the midst of challenges is a miraculous quality of life, and that's what God promises when we learn to trust and follow Him fully.

With God in control, we have nothing to fear. He is the Master of the universe. His wisdom is superior to ours in every way, and no situation is too complex or hopeless for Him to solve.

God has even provided a solution for our ongoing frailties and failings. As part of His great redemption, He offers con-

tinuing forgiveness and cleansing from all unrighteousness (1 John 1:9). We make mistakes—sometimes willfully violating His plan for us—but He welcomes our confession and honors it by restoring our fellowship and renewing our guidance.

Once we begin to experience the rewards of financial faithfulness, we never want to be without them. Our deepening trust in *God's* faithfulness intensifies our desire to stay within His will, resulting in perfect peace.

Many people have inherited or achieved financial independence: a level of wealth that requires no further work or income. But apart from Christ, they don't have freedom from anxiety; they have merely replaced one set of worries with another. They often fear:

- Loss of what they have accumulated

- Loss of meaningful relationships—fearing that others only care about what they have rather than who they are

- Loss of safety as their wealth makes them a target for theft or kidnapping

- Loss of grace from others, who jealously hold them to a higher standard because of their wealth

Being financially free, on the other hand, includes freedom from these fears as well as from the oppression of envy, covetousness, and greed.

Financial faithfulness is transformation—a process that requires God's power and our participation. It is synonymous with our definition of true financial faithfulness in the *Crown Money Map*™:

1. Knowing that God owns it all.

2. Finding contentment with what He provides.

3. Being free to be all He made you to be.

This is the big picture, the framework within which wealth and material possessions take their rightful place—not as ends but as means—in God's hands.

Steps to Cultivate Financial Faithfulness

Now it is time to outline the path. Since we're talking about transformation, you'll notice that some of our steps go well beyond mere money-management techniques.

1. TRANSFER OWNERSHIP.

Transferring ownership of every possession to God means acknowledging that He already owns them and that we will begin treating them accordingly. This includes more than just material possessions; it includes money, time, family, education, even earning potential for the future. This is essential to experience the Spirit-filled life in the area of finances (see Psalm 8:4-6).

There is no substitute for this step. If we believe we are the owners of even a single possession, then the events affecting that possession are going to affect our attitudes. God will not input His perfect will into our lives unless we first surrender our wills to Him.

However, if we make a total transfer of everything to God, He will demonstrate His ability. It is important to understand and accept God's conditions for His control (see Deuteronomy 5:32-33). God will keep His promise to provide our every need according to His perfect plan.

It is easy to say we will make a total transfer of everything to God, but it's not so easy to do. Our desire for control and our habit of self-management cause difficulty in consistently seeking God's will in the area of material things. But without a deep conviction that He is in control, we can never experience true financial faithfulness.

What a great relief it is to turn our burdens over to Him. Then, if something happens to the car, we can say, "Father, I gave this car to You; I've maintained it to the best of my ability, but I don't own it. It belongs to You, so do with it whatever You like." Then look for the blessing God has in store as a result of this attitude.

2. BECOME DEBT FREE.

God wants us to be free to serve Him without restriction. *"You were bought with a price; do not become slaves of men"* (1 Corinthians 7:23). *"The rich rules over the poor, and the borrower becomes the lender's slave"* (Proverbs 22:7).

Read *Debt and Bankruptcy*, another book in the *MoneyLife™ Basics Series*, for further information on this, including definitions and steps for getting out of debt. For most, this will involve sacrifice—at least initially—but the payoff is well worth it.

3. GIVE REGULARLY AND GENEROUSLY.

Every follower of Christ should establish tithing (10 percent of income) as a beginning point of giving and as a testimony to God's ownership. We can't say we have given total ownership to God if our actions don't back the claim.

It is through sharing that we bring His power in finances into focus. In every case, God wants us to give the first part to Him, but He also wants us to pay our creditors. This requires establishing a plan, and it will probably mean making sacrifices of wants and desires until all obligations are current.

We cannot sacrifice God's part—that is not our prerogative as faithful, obedient followers of Christ. Malachi 3:8-9 has strong words for those who "rob God." But then verses 10-12 describe His great blessing for those who tithe fully.

God, as the first giver, wants us to be like Him, and His economy rewards our generosity. *"Now this I say, he who sows sparingly will also reap sparingly, and he who sows bountifully will also reap bountifully"* (2 Corinthians 9:6).

Steps two and three combine to form an important conclusion. If, while en route to financial faithfulness, sacrifice becomes necessary—and it almost always does—our sacrifice must not come from God's or our creditor's share. We must choose areas within our other discretionary expenses to sacrifice. Consider it an opportunity to exercise faith in God's reward for our obedience.

4. ACCEPT GOD'S PROVISION.

To obtain financial peace, recognize and accept that God's provision is used to direct each of our lives. Often Christians lose sight of the fact that God's will can be accomplished through a withholding of funds; we think that He can direct us only by an abundance of money. But God does not choose for everyone to live in great abundance. This does not imply poverty, but it may mean that God wants us to be more responsive to His day-by-day control.

Followers of Christ must learn to live on what God provides and not give in to a driving desire for wealth or the pressure brought on by comparison with others. This necessitates planning our lifestyle within the provision God has supplied. When we are content to do this, God will always help us find a way.

5. KEEP A CLEAR CONSCIENCE.

Living with integrity means dealing with the past as well as the present. Part of becoming financially faithful requires gaining a clear conscience regarding past business practices and personal dealings. Sometimes, in addition to a changed attitude, our transformation means making restitution for situations where we have wronged someone.

Tim's story is a good example. Before he accepted Christ, he cheated someone out of some money. God convicted him about this and indicated that he should go and make restitution. He contacted the person, confessed what had been done, and offered to make it right. The person refused to forgive and also refused to take any money.

Tim's ego and pride were hurt until he realized that he had been both obedient and successful. His confession was not primarily for the offended person but for his own relationship with God. He had done exactly what God had asked, and God had forgiven him. Nothing further was required.

6. PUT OTHERS FIRST.

This does not imply being a door mat; it simply means that we shouldn't profit at the unfair expense of someone else. As is often the case, attitude is all-important.

7. MANAGE TIME PRIORITIES.

A workaholic might gain wealth at the expense of the family's relational needs, but wealth alone is no indicator of financial faithfulness. And wealth gained with wrong priorities is likely to vanish. *"Do not weary yourself to gain wealth, cease from your consideration of it. When you set your eyes on it, it is gone. For wealth certainly makes itself wings like an eagle that flies toward the heavens"* (Proverbs 23:4-5). Even if it doesn't vanish, it can't deliver the satisfaction it promises. Don't be deceived by overcommitment to business or the pursuit of wealth.

God's priorities for us are very clear.

Priority number one is to develop our relationship with Jesus Christ.

Priority number two is our family. This includes teaching them God's Word. And that requires quality time, something that can't exist without a sufficient quantity from which to flow.

Develop the habit of a regular time to study God's Word for yourself as well as a family time that acknowledges your commitment to each other and to God.

Turn off the television, have the children do their homework early, and begin to study the Bible together. Pray for each other and for those in need. Help your children become intercessors who can pray for others and expect God to answer.

Priority number three is your work, which God intends to be an opportunity for ministry and personal development in addition to providing an income.

Priority number four is church activities and other ministry. This does not imply that it is unimportant or can be neglected, but it keeps us from using church as an excuse to let higher priorities slide. If we observe priority number one, we will not neglect our church.

8. AVOID OVER-INDULGENCE.

Jesus said, *"If anyone wishes to come after Me, he must deny himself, and take up his cross daily and follow Me"* (Luke 9:23). Once again, this is about priorities. Who wins the contest between God's claim on your life and your own pursuit of pleasure?

In Philippians 3:18-19, Paul says that many live as the enemies of the cross of Christ, and he describes them by saying, *"Their destiny is destruction, their god is their stomach, and their glory is in their shame"* (NIV).

That sounds alarmingly like much of our culture, and it takes great effort to avoid being swept along with the current.

9. GET CHRISTIAN COUNSEL.

"Without consultation, plans are frustrated, but with many counselors they succeed" (Proverbs 15:22). God admonishes us to seek counsel and not to rely solely on our own resources. People are often frustrated in financial planning because they lack the necessary knowledge. A common but tragic response is to give up. Within the body of Christ, God has supplied those who have the ability to help in the area of finances. Seek Christian counselors.

To read more on what God says about handling money, go to Crown.org and click "Bible Tools."

Crown's mission is to provide you with help, hope, and insight as you seek to grow in financial faithfulness.

Stay Connected at Crown.org

With a comprehensive collection of online tools and resources, Crown.org will teach you how to make money, manage money, and ultimately fulfill God's purposes for your life.

God's wisdom will make a difference in your finances!

Resources

To Help You in Life and Money

Career Direct®

You have unlimited potential to be more, do more, and maximize your God-given talents and abilities. You are ready to exceed everyone's expectations.

Go to CareerDirectOnline.org to get started.

Crown Budgeting Solutions

Choose the Budgeting Solution That Fits Your Lifestyle

Paper

• Traditional option using paper, pen, and cash.

Software

• Computer software option for your PC or Mac.

Online and Mobile

• Web and Mobile option available anytime, anywhere.

For details, go to Crown.org/BudgetingSolutions

MoneyLife™ BASICS SERIES BOOKS

Pocket-Sized Help and Hope

◀ Learn the foundational basics of investing and insurance

ISBN 978-1-56427-253-9

SPENDING PLAN SOLUTIONS

Spending Plan/Budgeting
Major Purchases-Houses and Cars

[MONEYLIFE™ BASICS SERIES]

ISBN 978-1-56427-252-2

▲ Create a successful spending plan, and plan for major purchases like homes and automobiles

DEBT AND BANKRUPTCY

Debt and Credit
Bankruptcy
Gambling/Lotteries

MONEYLIFE™ BASICS SERIES

ISBN 978-1-56427-251-5

◀ Understand the pitfalls of debt, the ins and outs of bankruptcy, and the dangers of gambling

To learn more about the entire series, contact your local book retailer or go to Crown.org